MW00917588

RELAUNCH YOUR NOVEL

BREATHE LIFE INTO YOUR BACKLIST

CHRIS FOX

Copyright © 2017 Chris Fox
All rights reserved.
ISBN: 1548299170
ISBN-13: 978-1548299170

To every indie who has ever helped a fellow author.
We are stronger together.

CONTENTS

INTRODUCTION

5,000 Words Per Hour, my first book for writers, came out in June of 2015, just over two years ago. When I wrote that book, I worked at a startup and wrote on the side. I rode the bus to work, cranking out as many words as I could while I bounced around in my seat.

That habit allowed me to produce eight books in sixteen months, not easy with a 60+ hour a week day job (something many of you can relate to). It was one of the most brutal things I've ever had to do, but in the end it freed me. I've been a full-time author for a little over a year, and I make more money than I ever did with software.

That's only possible because I now have 22 books in my backlist. An author's backlist is the lifeblood of her career, the constant stream of revenue that will keep her rent or mortgage paid while she works on the next big release. It's the money that keeps coming in when he takes a year off to sail around the world, or if he takes time off from writing.

Unfortunately, as far as I could tell, there was no book out there teaching backlist management. I've read stacks of books for authors; while a few offer some general tips, none present a comprehensive system for turning your backlist into a money factory.

So I wrote one. Within, you'll find everything I know about keeping my books afloat, and about relaunching titles that never received the right kind of opportunity for success when I first launched them. The beauty of being an author is that your intellectual property can be used however you want, and the fact that a book didn't do well on the first go around doesn't mean that you can't still sell thousands of copies.

I use my own backlist for many examples, but have also included case studies from other successful authors. These authors write in a variety of genres, but there are commonalities in their relaunches that will help you get your backlist producing the kind of income you want it to.

That, folks, is the holy grail. I know the title of this book is *Relaunch Your Novel*, and you're absolutely going to do that. But the real takeaway, the one that will make you money for the rest of your life? That's the *Breathe Life Into Your Backlist* part.

As in all my books, I try to keep me out of it. But, inevitably, some people want to know a little about the author. Please be advised that the next several paragraphs may contain pompous windbaggery.

Who is Chris Fox and can he really teach this stuff?

I published my first novel in October of 2014. At that time, I had the advantage of working at a San Francisco startup. Not only did this pay me very well; it also meant I was on the bleeding edge of technological development.

This allowed me to predict where publishing was going to go, and to get out ahead of the rest of the crowd. I funneled several thousand dollars into launching *No Such Thing As Werewolves*, and the book paid back those production costs by January of 2015. I was floored.

My little book had made over $4,000 in a single

month, due largely to the audio release. The light-bulb went on in my head. What if I had ten books out? Or twenty? How much would I be earning every month?

Unfortunately, at that time I didn't understand the concept of a book launch. I assumed that sales would remain steady for many months, possibly even years. I didn't understand that yesterday's hot new release is today's bargain bin leftovers.

I eagerly cranked out a second novel, and then a third. I ventured into non-fiction. By late 2015, I understood how the sales curve worked, and knew that fiction has a big burst at release, then fades into a long tail. So I focused on releasing as many books as possible. I cranked out a fourth novel. Then a fifth. As of this writing, I have 12 full-length novels out.

At some point along the way I got tired. It felt like sprinting on a treadmill, always rushing to get the next new release out. If I stopped, even for a moment, my income fell sharply. I found this out the hard way when I didn't put out a novel for six months.

And yes, I realize some of you are goggling, thinking that putting out a novel every six months is faster than light speed. Go read *Six Figure Author* if you want my stance on that. =p

I figured that there had to be a better way. Why did my old series stop selling? What could I do to keep them selling? Facebook ads? Kindle Countdown Deals? Permafree? What was the solution to ensure a stream of sales?

I didn't know, so I started experimenting. I did all the things. Some worked moderately well. Most didn't work at all. But every once in a while something would just click, and I'd sell a bunch of books. The more I experimented, the better the results. Eventually, my backlist income stabilized. I was still having 5 figure months, despite not having put out a new novel for half a year.

I cannot stress enough the significance of this change. The single largest thing I wrestle with as an author is the constant pressure to crank out books as quickly as possible. The knowledge that my backlist lets me slow down to a manageable pace reduced my stress by about a million percent.

Today, I'm still a six-figure author. I'm still cranking out a ton of books, and most of those books are written to market. But, more than ever, I'm more concerned about my backlist than I am about my new releases.

After you read this book, I hope you are, too.

-Chris

THE ASSESSMENT

If you're reading this, you should have at least one book out (a novel, or a non-fiction book). Maybe you have ten. Or twenty. But you need to have at least one. If you don't, your money and time are better spent elsewhere. I have five other books in this series, all of which will probably help you more than this one.

The goal of *this* book is to transform your back-list into an automatic money-making machine, whether you're the one-book guy or the ten-book gal. So you kind of need that backlist to get started.

In both cases, the following scenario is probably very familiar:

You launched a book, you had some sales, and then the book slowly sank into oblivion. Sales decay over time; it's a sad fact of author life. Now, if you don't run a promotion, your once mighty book moves barely any copies at all. The older it is, the less that sales line moves.

Or—and this is far more likely for most of us—you launched a book and didn't have any sales. A few of your friends bought it at 99 cents, you ran a couple promotions, and now you have eight reviews and a seven-figure rank on Amazon.

In both cases, those books are not pulling their weight in your backlist. For most authors, we simply ignore those books. They were flops, and we reason that our time is better spent working on a new release with the potential to sell better. Subconsciously, we dissociate ourselves from books that fail. Focusing on new releases lets us avoid past failures.

I'm not suggesting you shouldn't be working on that new release. You absolutely should. What I'm saying is that you should do *both*.

The beauty of this industry is that you can experiment constantly. A few simple changes might breathe life into all your books, turning two or three sales a day into twenty. Or a full relaunch might give it a chance to break into the Amazon top 1,000.

But before either of those are possible, you need to understand why your book(s) aren't selling.

The Assessment

This is the really ugly part, the part that makes us squirm in our chairs, or close the book and go back to watching *Game of Thrones*. It's also the most necessary part. You can't skip this if you want to relaunch.

Relaunching your novel(s) requires brutal self-honesty. The process begins by assessing your own book or series, and determining why it failed to meet reader expectations. In some cases, you may have made very few mistakes. In most cases, however, you're going to cringe as you identify tons of mistakes. I know I have.

If you've had books flop, don't worry. We'll be using some of my books as (very painful) examples. I've made nearly every mistake that can be made, and lived to tell about it. You will (or already have) too.

The real trick to succeeding long term is separating yourself from the writing. You are looking at what you have produced with a critical eye, so that you can flag things to work on to make the next thing you create better.

Determining why your book failed begins,

believe it or not, with an understanding of genres. Does your book fit where you placed it? Let's find out.

What Genre Is Your Novel?

Before we get started we need to **properly** identify your book's niche. I stress properly, because it's very possible to be wrong about where your book is placed. Especially if you have one of those genre-bending books we all love to write.

My first novel was called *No Such Thing As Werewolves,* and I touted it as—wait for it—a genre-bending book, aka code for "I have no idea what genre to put this in."

The title and cover suggest horror, or possibly urban fantasy. It's a big werewolf standing next to a pyramid, with creepy red typography. Unfortunately, the book is about as far from horror as you can get. There are horror elements, but that's not really the tone. The tone is more about triumphing over the impossible. Guess what genre that belongs to? Not horror, that's for sure.

What I'd written was a thriller. The problem is,

you'd never know that from the title or cover. It's not until you read the blurb that you realize there are thriller elements—and if you don't like werewolves, odds are good you never got as far as reading the blurb. I did a masterful job of mis-marketing my book.

This was discouraging, but I knew there had to be a solution. I'd done a lot of reading, and knew there were series similar to mine. One of the closest was *The Atlantis Gene,* by A.G. Riddle. His book was branded as a science fiction (SF) thriller. It looked like an SF thriller. It was titled like an SF thriller.

If I were assessing my book as a horror novel, I'd give the cover and title a big thumbs up. But I'm not. And as an SF thriller, the cover is a total fail.

Genre is the lens through which you view every part of your book, which is why we're starting there. If you market your book to the wrong genre, you're all but guaranteeing failure. It's vital that you understand what genre you want to market to, even if your book can be placed in several categories. You need to ground your relaunch in the genre you think best fits your book. Only then can you go through the assessment steps below.

Step 1- The Cover

I beat this to death in *Write to Market* and *Six Figure Author*, but it needs to be mentioned again. Your cover is absolutely vital to any book's success.

"But wait," some of you are saying, "there are books that blow up and have crap covers." That's true, but *your* chances of success are exponentially lower with a poor cover. They are likewise enhanced when you have the right cover.

Just having a beautiful cover isn't enough, though. As mentioned above, the cover needs to fit the genre. As you'll see in the next chapter, I have a series of amazing covers that are absolutely wrong for the genre those books are in. They were a great idea, but if I really want that series to succeed I need to replace them all.

So how about you? Is your cover as good or better than the top sellers in your genre(s)? Is the typography crisp, clear, and well branded? Does the subject matter both intrigue the reader and subtly inform them about the genre in a way that makes them think of similar books?

All important questions. Right now, all you'll need to do is think about the answers. Don't worry about what to do just yet; you're only making notes right now.

Step 2- The Title

Titles are hard, and sometimes even harder to assess. Does your title convey the right emotional resonance with your targeted genre? That's a tough question to answer.

No Such Thing As Werewolves tells you that there's almost certainly werewolves involved. *The Atlantis Gene* tells you that there's some sort of genetic link to Atlantis. *The Martian* plays on your preconceived notions of what a Martian is, turning it on its head.

Shorter titles can do this too, like *Constitution* by Nick Webb. Most military buffs will immediately recognize the reference to one of the greatest naval vessels in American history. The association will change by genre, but your title represents a chance to pack a lot into very few words.

So how about your title? What does it say about the series / genre? Anything? Or did you pick it because it's a reference to something in the plot?

As you'll hear in the case study in the next chapter, changing a title might be a very necessary part of a re-branding your novel.

Step 3- The Blurb

After cover and title, the most important part of selling books is the product description (blurb). I cannot overstate the importance of your sales copy. A poor blurb will kill a book nearly as quickly as a bad cover. You have exactly one sentence to grab your reader, and your pitch needs to be tailored to your genre.

Your cozy mystery, gripping thriller, and terrifying horror novel all hit different emotional notes. Your blurb needs to capture those notes, or you are going to struggle to sell books.

Looking at your book's blurb, does it do those things? Does it capture the genre, and excite the reader? How does it compare to other blurbs in your genre?

Here are the first sentence or two from three different blurbs (reprinted with permission):

The Galaxy is a Dumpster Fire. - *Legionnaire*, Nick Cole & Jason Anspach

Starting an interstellar security consulting company was supposed to be easy. Rade got his ex-military teammates together and they pooled their savings to buy a ship and six mechs. - *Bug Hunt*, Isaac Hooke

Bill Ryder was a dateless geek, but then he met a girl to die for. So he did. - *Bill The Vampire*, Rick Gualtieri

Notice how in each case you get a sense of the genre. You know that the galaxy is a rough place, after just one sentence. In the second example, you know that we've got mechs, and that we're likely to have a down-on-their-luck crew struggling to keep their heads above water.

The third example tells you this is going to be funny, and invites the reader to the third and fourth sentences where we learn that Bill doesn't stop being a loser just because he's now a vampire.

Does your blurb do these things? Does it fit the

others in your genre? If you're not sure, that's totally okay. Find people succeeding in your genre, and ask them for their take. Post your blurb in writing communities and ask for help tweaking it. Workshop the crap out of it, until it's perfect.

For now, though, don't worry about fixing your blurb. Just note if you think it's in need of work, and if so how much.

Step 4- Branding

So what is branding exactly? You want typography and covers that compliment each other, so that it's clear when someone sees the books that they're in the same series. You want people to say "Oh, that's a Deathless book."

That's just half the equation, though. Your series brand should feed into your author brand. I want people to recognize a Chris Fox book, even if it's in a brand-new series. This is usually done through consistent typography, though using the same cover artist helps.

Note that this only applies to series in the same genre. If you write, say, erotic romance and children's books, then you should consider using a pen name for one of them. Each will have its own separate brand, and that brand should be consistent.

The idea is that every book on any given pen name should reinforce the other books. Does your book do that? If not, why do you think that is? Add it to your notes, because we'll be changing that during the relaunch.

Step 5- The Writing

The literary writers among us are going to wince. The *actual writing* is #5 in order of importance, because quite frankly unless the first three things (and to a lesser extent, the first four) are in order no one will ever see the inside of your book.

HOWEVER (yes I meant to both bold and capitalize that word), that doesn't mean the writing isn't vital. Not necessarily your prose—though the better that is the more fans you'll attract—but the storytelling. Story structure is far, far more important to your continued success than grammar or prose.

I realize this is controversial. I still get one star reviews on *Write To Market* for saying it was okay to publish with a few typos. Here's the thing though, and I say this having sold a *lot* of books: Most readers will forgive the occasional typo. **They will not forgive a boring story.**

Note that I'm not arguing in favor of typos. You want a clean book—as clean as you can possibly make it. What I'm saying is that understanding how to write a compelling story is critical, more so than perfection in prose. If you have to sacrifice one for the other, make sure you do not sacrifice story.

Go back and reread the first three chapters of the book you're attempting to relaunch. How's the writing? Does the prose still work? Is the pacing good? Does it fit the genre where you've placed it? Does it pull you into the story?

Jot down the answers, and be brutally honest. It's okay to admit that it needs a total rewrite, and it's not arrogant to say that the writing is good. Judge for yourself—but if you've got a substantial number of reviews, listen to them as well. What do they say about your writing?

Are there common themes, good or bad? Jot them down. It's hard, but this will not only help you make more money from your backlist. It will also make you a better writer.

Step 6- Exposure

Think back to your launch. What did you do, *exactly*? Did you use social media? Which? How about book promotion sites? Again, which ones? Did you just upload it to Amazon and cross your fingers? Be honest, and jot it all down. Include what worked and what didn't.

Why? We're trying to determine how much exposure your book had. If you pulled out all the stops and ran a thousand dollars in ads, yet still only have 12 reviews...Houston, we have a problem. If you simply had very little exposure, having only a few reviews is normal, and will not reflect on the quality of the book.

When we relaunch, exposure will be critical, and our short term goal is simply to make sure we get more exposure than we did on the initial launch.

So why isn't exposure higher on the list? Why does it come last? Isn't getting eyes on your work the most important thing that you can do?

No. No, it isn't. If you get 40,000 people to see your book, but you have a terrible cover, an unreadable blurb, and embarrassing writing...well, you're not going to sell very many books.

If, on the other hand, every other step is *nailed*, then when you drive eyes to your book you're going to sell a boatload of copies. Get everything else right, then tell the world about it.

My Usual Note About Exercises

As with all the books in this series, all exercises are gathered into an appendix at the end of the book. If you want to read straight through, feel free to do so. If that's your intention, please ignore the multiple guilt trips sprinkled throughout the book.

Exercise #1- This one won't surprise you. All the questions we asked earlier? Get out a sheet of paper, open a Word document, or get out your tablet. Answer all questions with as much detail as you can. Understand that some of the answers will require you to spend time researching. Or reading.

Try to spend at least a few minutes on each question, until you are satisfied you've answered it as completely as possible. Spend longer if you need to.

If this is something you don't yet feel comfortable doing, read the next chapter. My case study gives context on how you complete an assessment.

Bonus: Repeat this exercise for each of the books in a series you want to relaunch. Over time, we're going to relaunch them all. Understanding what you have to work with for your entire backlist will be very helpful as you read the rest of this book.

2

CASE STUDY: DEATHLESS

Throughout this book, I've included case studies to illustrate the principles we've just gone over. In this case, I want to show you how to conduct an assessment as explained in the last chapter.

Let's take a look at one of my books, *No Such Thing As Werewolves*. It's a perfect example for relaunch, because I did a lot wrong. It was my very first novel, and I made almost every mistake you can. I broke two of the three cardinal rules:

- Poor packaging (Blurb, cover, title)
- Poor content (the writing)
- Improperly identified audience

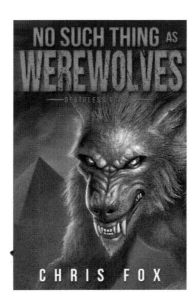

The Story of *Deathless*

Deathless is a genre-bending thriller—horror, science fiction, and apocalyptic mystery. It was my attempt to make something unique, and I succeeded. *Deathless* is unlike anything else out there. That makes it very, very difficult to sell.

People who gave the series a try absolutely love the books, and I get emailed constantly for sequels. But I don't sell a lot of new copies. When I recently launched *The Great Pack*, the fans all bought it, then the book sank quickly into obscurity. The book ranks don't skyrocket like they do when I put out military science fiction like *Destroyer* or *Behind The Lines*.

After launch, *Deathless* sales die back to meh levels, then slowly decline to a flatline. The ads become less effective over time. Everything I do to prop the series up fails to *keep* it up. Does any of that sound familiar?

I fell into the number one and number three trap. I had no clue who my audience was, and my covers reflect that. I got artwork that I loved, and I gave the books titles I thought were funny. *No Such Thing As Werewolves. No Mere Zombie. Vampires Don't Sparkle.* I laid it on pretty thick, which is a problem because the books are not comedies, as the titles suggest.

The series sold fairly well when I launched the first book. People loved the werewolf and the pyramid under the moonlight. I had a small but devoted group of werewolf fans, and they were rabid (see what I did there?) about the series. They told friends and family, and I got a lot of fan mail.

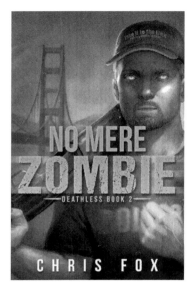

I released book two, and *bam*: here's a picture of a zombie holding a shotgun, standing next to the Golden Gate Bridge. My small but loyal following all bought the book and loved it. Those sales nudged the book high enough that the zombie crowd found it. The zombie crowd is massive, but they have very specific conventions that smart authors observe. I broke every one of those conventions—meaning this wasn't really a zombie series, as those zombie fans told me in droves.

The third book introduced vampires, so I've got this dude in a suit standing next to Stonehenge. It's a cool cover, but it in no way resembles either of the previous two books. Vampire fans also have some pretty specific conventions they like followed, and I broke all of those, just like I did for zombies.

I tried marketing this to the werewolf crowd, but they aren't the right audience. I tried marketing to the zombie crowd, but they weren't the right place either. Vampires? Yeah, no.

Yet that's what my covers screamed. People who bought my books were expecting one type of story, but were in fact getting something completely different. Horror fans didn't get the horror ending they wanted. Urban fantasy (UF) fans weren't getting the magic they wanted, though a surprising number of UF fans stuck with the series.

Other Problems

My blurb, thankfully, is compelling. The writing itself, though, is not—at least not the first quarter of the book. *No Such Thing As Werewolves* was my first novel, and the pacing is terrible. People mention over and over in reviews that the beginning is slow. If you want proof, go take a look at the sample. You'll see exactly what I mean.

If I want *Deathless* to soar, the writing could really be improved. Admitting this might have been difficult once upon a time, but by this point I've removed ego from the process. There are lots of problems in my first series, from a botched ending to inaccuracies about firearms to my serious aversion to commas.

A full relaunch for *Deathless* would mean re-editing at least the first full novel, and possibly the first three. These books are long, so we're talking about 400,000 words of re-writing. That's a massive undertaking that would probably take me several months, if I wanted to do it right. There are a million tiny concerns, from breaking Whispersync with the changes, to how changes I make in this book might ripple through the sequels.

At this stage, I'm not deciding whether or not that work is warranted. It might be. It might not. That will come later. For now, I'm just diagnosing the problems.

Possible Plans of Action

During my research, I discovered trends among the people who'd left five-star reviews. The crowd who most enjoyed the books all described it as a thriller. They used words like *fast-paced*. Action and Adventure. Thrilling. Couldn't put the book down. Lost sleep. These cropped up over and over.

To them, this series was *Indiana Jones* meets *Stargate*. These people generally had no preconceived notions about werewolves or zombies, or were at least willing to entertain my reimagining.

These people like Michael Bay movies. They enjoy a breakneck pace and world-sweeping revelations. They liked my mix of science and history connecting all these ancient myths.

Do my covers say anything at all like that to you? They sure don't. They're wonderful covers, but they advertise completely the wrong genres. I have werewolves and vampires and zombies, but my series isn't really about those things.

Egyptian gods, the origins of mankind, and a long vanished culture—*that's* what my series is about. Looming over all of it, is a solar apocalypse. A coronal mass ejection that will wipe out all technology. Those are the real hooks.

As stated above, my audience is people who don't normally read about vampires or werewolves or zombies. They like thrillers, and are okay with a supernatural bent to it. They like things to be explained logically, and hate having their suspension of disbelief broken. They roll their eyes at the idea of werewolves...unless you explain, using convincing pseudo-science, how it's possible that they can exist.

Then those people get *really* interested. When you use accurate history, tying it together to prove that an earlier species could have existed on our planet, you make lifelong fans. You scratch an itch with a very specific person, a person who would never dream of picking up a book with a werewolf cover. That screams horror, and that person isn't interested in reading about werewolves and silver bullets.

The people who would pick up that cover cling to a set of rules about their favorite supernatural creatures, and they didn't necessarily care about ancient history. Some were really angry when I did things like give werewolves superpowers. That didn't make sense to them, even if I offered up a scientific explanation. Some didn't like that my zombies were intelligent, even though that too was explained meticulously. Then I threw in aliens and super heroes, both explained just as convincingly as the zombies.

Those thriller lovers? They can't get enough. They love the convincing explanations. For them, that's the pay off. How is Chris going to get me to accept that aliens fit in his world?

Clearly, I need to reach that thriller audience. I know that they love the book as it's written. So how do I jettison the wrong audience, and attract the right one?

I need to transform my series into one that thriller fans will pick up.

The Transformation

If I really want to sell this series, I need to completely rebrand it. I need to do away with the cheesy titles—and, as much as I love the covers, they have to go too.

Instead of a werewolf, the first book might have a shot of earth. In the background, the sun will be flaring and a wave of energy is about to wash over the earth. The title might simply be *Deathless*, or *The First Conspiracy*, or something equally thriller-ish. If I go with *Deathless*, subsequent books will also have single-word titles.

The categories will change to Thrillers, and Action and Adventure. The books I target with my ads will also see a dramatic shift. I'll aim the series at an entirely different market. Same content, brand new packaging.

Instead of seeing this really scary werewolf, you'll see an evocative apocalyptic thriller. The people who would consider reading the former is much smaller than the people who would read the latter. More importantly, the second audience has proven that they enjoy the series more.

Final Analysis

Retooling *Deathless* would require more time than I can afford, and would represent a significant investment of cash, too. So I'm not going to give it the full treatment. I understand the problems the series has, and the day will come when I have time to address them—most likely when I'm ready to sit down and write the next *Deathless* book.

Until then, I need to work with what I have. I took a careful look at the ads I was running, and realized that I simply couldn't make these books profitable at their current prices ($2.99 for the first and $3.99 for the sequels). So I raised the prices a dollar across the board.

Sales didn't change at all; I just made more money. Suddenly, my ads were profitable. That simple change will have a huge long-term impact.

I'm not leaving it there, though. I'm a huge fan of experiments, because everything is theoretical until you test it. If you look at my Deathless covers, you'll notice that one is quite unlike the rest.

Wait a minute. That isn't a werewolf or a zombie. It's a beautiful priestess in prehistoric garb. She's got a golden staff on her shoulder, and it looks Egyptian. Yup, there's a pyramid behind her.

Think about what this cover says that the others do not. There are no automatic negative tropes like werewolves or vampires. There is simply a mysterious woman and a pyramid.

If I back this up with the one word title *Deathless*, I think action and adventure fans might respond well to it. I'm reasonably sure UF fans will, since this was the artwork used on my short story *The First Ark*. I saw how they responded.

I'm testing this by launching a brand new *Deathless* box set, which includes the first three volumes. The titles of the individual novels will not change, but will be mentioned only once, at the bottom of the blurb.

If I'm right, this will push past the stigma that thriller readers have about werewolves and zombies. Since the book has a new Amazon Standard Identification Number (ASIN), it will once again be on the hot new releases list at Amazon. With some smart marketing, the box set could re-ignite interest in the series.

Or, it could flop. Even a flop is likely to turn a small profit, since I'm using artwork I already own and books I've already written. Either way, I will learn about my readers. If the experiment fails, I'll use the results to conduct another experiment.

The beauty of this lightweight approach is that I don't have to invest much time or money. I can try it quickly, and see how it goes. If it does well, I can give more time and attention to relaunching *Deathless*.

If it flops, I can concoct another experiment.

The Assessment

Below you'll find my report card for Deathless. These are real world notes, scribbled as I completed my assessment.

Step 1- The Cover
Grade: C

Covers do not properly convey genre. Werewolf and zombie say horror. Werewolves and zombies are too dissimilar from tropes. Readers of UF do not like the addition of technological elements, or aliens. Readers of horror are split, many upset over my take on werewolves or zombies. Readers of thrillers love it.

Step 2- The Title
Grade: C

Totally wish I could go back to 2014 to smack myself. I thought these titles were so funny, and now they're hamstringing the series. Bad Chris. Need to brainstorm new set of thriller titles.

Step 3- The Blurb
Grade: A

Blurb is tight. It hits the right notes and has proven very effective. The elements fit a thriller, so this is spot on. Blurbs for books 2-3 could use some tightening.

Step 4- Branding
Grade: D

Terrible. Like really terrible. The covers are obviously in the same series, but that series is reminiscent of Goosebumps. Not cool to thriller readers. The first book appealed strongly to werewolf fans. The second and third lost them.

Step 5- The Writing
Grade: B-

Ouch. First 20 chapters could be cut down to six without losing anything. The pacing is all wrong. Could convey so much more in shorter first act. Also: commas, man. Jesus, why did you hate them so badly?

Ending of book two is bad enough that it warrants changing. Other than that, though, the first couple books have lots of great moments and emotional pulls.

Step 6- Exposure
Grade: B+

I used classic shotgun advertising in the beginning, but I did a lot of it. A lot of eyes saw the first book, but I never adequately advertised the sequels.

Final Assessment

I can't afford to do much with the series right now. I really want to write book five, and when I allocate time to do that it will also be time to rebrand this entire series. Until then, I need to strengthen my SF author brand.

3

DOES RELAUNCHING MAKE SENSE?

You did the exercise at the end of chapter one, right? The one we demonstrated in the case study chapter? You didn't just turn the page. I mean, it's cool if you did (it's not cool). I'm not trying to guilt you. (I totally am.)

So now you're staring at a pile of notes about your book. What do you do with them? You analyze them to determine what you think would be required to successfully relaunch your book, and then you conduct an experiment.

That relaunch can take many forms, or you may decide that you don't want to relaunch at all. Maybe instead you end up tweaking the front and back matter, and the blurb, and then running a few promotions.

Or you could rebuild an entire series from the

ground up, like Bryan Cohen did. In both cases, your motivator should be **return on investment**. Not just your investment of money, but your investment of time.

If it's going to take a year to rewrite your four-book series, is that a wise use of your valuable writing time? Maybe. Only you can make that call.

Calculating ROI

Let's start with the most tangible asset, money.

- How much did your book originally cost to produce?
- What will it cost to make the changes you need to make?

It's okay to ballpark some of this, if you haven't tracked your finances. Ideally, you should know how much you spent on covers, editing, advertising, and any other promotion. Total all that up; if you're unable to, then make a reasonable guess.

If you're wide (published on all the ebook retailers) this will take a little more detective work, but add up how much money you've made from your book. Include paperbacks, audio, and any other distribution channel you've made money on. What's the total? Has your book made a profit, or are you in the red?

Now, how much would it cost to get new cover(s)? How much would you allocate to advertising? How much do you need to sell to pay for those changes?

The answers are important, because at the end of the day all your books need to be profitable. If they are not—if they are a big, black money pit—then we need to be realistic. Some books need to be unpublished. Not every book can be saved.

It's far more important to focus on the ones with the best ROI. For example, my *Void Wraith* trilogy is still selling well a year after publication because I put a lot of my advertising budget behind it. I put my advertising budget behind it because the sell-through is so high.

I also wrote a sequel trilogy, because I knew read-through would be high. The ROI is higher than any other series, so that's where my time and attention goes.

How Do You Calculate Read-Through?

Read-through is, quite simply, how many people who've read one of your books will go on to buy the next book. This can be linear, like each book in a series, or it can be a bunch of standalone books in the same genre (like the one you're holding).

Is someone who bought one of your books likely to buy the next? There's no way to get a completely accurate answer, but we can take some basic measurements to give us some idea. This is far, far easier to do if you have a series.

How many copies of book one did you sell in the last 30 days? How many copies did you sell of book two? And book three, through however many you have?

Take book two, and divide by book one. Repeat this for the rest of the books in your series. This is your read-through, or the percentage of people who bought book one that stuck around to read your entire series.

- Book 1: 50 copies
- Book 2: 42 copies
- Book 3: 32 copies
- Book 4: 51 copies

These numbers come from my *Deathless* series.

No Such Thing As Werewolves sells about 2 copies a day. Book two has an 84% read-through rate. Book three has a 64% read-through rate. Book four, on the other hand, we can't calculate. Since this book came out recently, it's outselling the first book in the series.

In this case, I calculate it based on book three. After the new-release dust settles, I'm guessing that *The Great Pack* will have around a 60% read-through. I'll use that estimate when calculating how much I'll earn for a sale of the entire series. By understanding read-through, I can figure out almost to the penny how much I'll earn for every person who purchases the first *Deathless* book.

It works like this. Take the royalties you'd earn, and multiply it by the read-through percentage:

- Book 1- $2.80
- Book 2- $2.94 (84% of the $3.50 I earn for a sale)
- Book 3- $2.24 (64% of the $3.50)
- Book 4- $2.10 (Based on my theoretical 60% number)

Total: $10.08

For every person who buys *No Such Thing As*

Werewolves, I'll make about $10. That goes up to about $12 if they borrow it using Kindle Unlimited. Those two numbers are critical, because now I know if I'm losing money when advertising.

This number is also important because it tells us how many copies of book one we need to sell in order to earn back the production costs we calculated above. If you are already $1,200 in the hole, and it's going to cost you $1,200 more to get new covers, plus say $300 in launch advertising, we now need to make $2,700 just to break even.

I need to sell 270 copies of *No Such Thing As Werewolves* to do that. If I had eight books instead of four, I'd probably only need to sell about 150. This is why having a deep backlist is so important. The deeper our sales funnels, the easier it is to break even, and then to make a profit.

If you only have one book at $3.99, you earn $2.80 a sale, versus my $10. You need to be four times as efficient in your advertising, or dramatically reduce your costs.

What If I Don't Have a Series?

Tracking read-through for standalone books is a

nightmare. Trust me, I feel your pain. This book you're reading is part of a six book "series." But it's not a series, not really. People don't start with book one and go right to book two. They cherry pick the book they think is most useful, and maybe they pick up a second or third one. Some people buy them all.

Sales come from podcast interviews, random tweets, blog posts, and a ton of other sources. This makes calculating sell-through very difficult, but I can still measure general trends. *5,000 Words Per Hour* is something you can read in two hours.

Most people do exactly that, and tend to pick another book within 48 hours. If I have a big promotion for *5,000 Words Per Hour*, the sales of all other books in the series will tick upwards one to two days later. It's not perfect, but it's something I can replicate.

However, since I can't quantify it, I don't count on it. I don't calculate read-through when advertising this series, and instead make each book be profitable by itself. That makes advertising much more challenging, but also ensures I don't lose money on ads.

What If I have a Series and My Read-Through Sucks?

If your read-through from book one to book two is under 50%, then you might have a problem with the writing. I say "might," because there are a lot of reasons why sales of book one can be much higher than book two. If you ran any sort of promotion during the 30-day window, like a Kindle Countdown Deal, then your numbers are going to be skewed. Many people buy books on sale, and then never read them.

You need to measure read-through during a normal humdrum month; if you can't find one, lower the time increment to a week.

If your sell-through still sucks? Then we've got a problem. There are many possible causes, but the most likely one is that your writing in those books simply wasn't good enough. For whatever reason people didn't decide to move on to book two.

This could be bad pacing, unlikable characters, or a host of other problems we've all wrestled with at some stage. If you see a trend in your reviews talking about an aspect of your writing, listen. It's very possible you need to improve in that area.

Fixing Your Craft

It might be that you simply need to get a book on the area of craft where you are weakest. If you're especially new, or there are many complaints about the quality of your writing, then turning to a professional might be the best way to go.

I was inordinately proud of my first novel, but dozens of reviews highlighted flaws in my writing. That broke my heart, and at first I didn't want to accept that they were right. Then, I finally got over my pride.

Hiring a writing coach was expensive, but was worth every penny and more. I learned about characterization, rising tension, and proper internal conflict. About it being okay for my protagonists to fight amongst themselves from time to time.

Alida held up a giant mirror, and over my next three novels I received an intense education. I improved immensely. You know what? It was one of the most painful things I've ever done. Having her tell me how terrible my writing was...it was demoralizing.

I got through it by reminding myself of something vital. *We are not the writing.* This book that you're relaunching? It isn't you. If your writing isn't up to par, so what? Figure out why, then improve. If you need to hire someone to help you do that, then hire them. If you can't afford it, become a better self-editor. Hustle. Find a way.

I've had one friend trade computer programming skills in exchange for a professional edit. I've had another pay using virtual assistant work. If you can't spare the money, don't let it stop you. Find a way to get whatever resource you need, be it a coach or just a great YouTube series about writing.

Exercise #2- Calculate ROI for the book / series you'd like to relaunch. How many copies do you need to sell to get this book into the black? If you're already in the black, how much do you need to make in order to consider this relaunch a success?

Bonus: Repeat this process for your entire backlist. Yeah, that can be a lot of work. It's totally worth it.

4

AUTHOR BRAND

A launch is about far more than just money, or even time. Before you invest either you need to ask a critical question. Does the book you want to relaunch fit your author brand? Will promoting it draw the kind of fans who will read the books you are writing *right now*?

If the answer is yes, rock on. But if it's no? FULL STOP.

We mentioned author brand earlier, and it may not be clear yet what that means. Put simply: if you're a science fiction author, then relaunching your standalone thriller does not fit your author brand. You can do it, but it isn't going to reinforce your brand; it's going to muddy it.

The biggest reason I'm not making *Deathless* more of a priority is because it does not fit my author brand. I'm actively trying to cultivate a science fiction audience, because those books are half the length and sell ten times the copies.

I love writing both, but one of them will actively further my career. One of them can wait until I can spare the time. For that reason, I'm launching two more science fiction trilogies this year. Then and only then will I write the next *Deathless* book.

Author branding determines my priority.

If the Relaunch Makes Money, Why Does Anything Else Matter?

Let's say your relaunch goes amazingly well, and you sell 10,000 copies in the first month. Yay, right? Maybe.

If you've built a platform as a mystery author, and you have a breakout steamy erotica, that's going to cause more problems than it's worth—unless you want to switch over to writing steamy erotica, in which case, goodbye mystery.

Every new science fiction book I publish reinforces my brand, and makes relaunching my backlist titles more effective and profitable. When I released *Behind The Lines* last month, it sold more copies in the first week than all my *Deathless* titles put together for the last six months.

I put out *Hold The Line* a week later, and the last book in the trilogy came out on June 23rd. Those books, as we'll examine later, reinforce my brand. They sell copies of all my other books, reinforcing each other. *Deathless*, unfortunately, doesn't.

I could relaunch the series, but I couldn't *capitalize on the launch momentum*. I'd get a quick flash of income, versus long term sustainable growth—the kind of growth that comes from establishing an easily recognizable brand.

So, What's Your Author Brand?

Are you a science fiction author? A non-fiction author? A romance author? What do you most enjoy writing, so much that you're willing to keep writing it for the next several years?

I've switched genres too many times, and now have two incomplete series in a genre that doesn't sell enough to warrant writing more of those books. I made mistakes, and I'm correcting them by honing in on my author brand.

What is that, exactly? Space Opera and Space

Fantasy. Everything I write for the rest of this year will follow that theme, yielding a total of nine science fiction novels this year. Every book strengthens that author brand, attracting more readers.

If I take a break to write an epic fantasy, my existing fan base isn't likely to buy it. Worse, writing that fantasy will create a second audience, one unlikely to read my science fiction. I've learned this the hard way. Most readers don't follow authors. They follow series.

Even Jim Butcher, who has sold many millions of *Dresden Files* books, had a hard time driving people to his steampunk series. *Cinder Spires* sold a tiny fraction of the *Dresden Files*, underperforming every other book Butcher has released.

His author brand? The creator of Harry Dresden. Like it or not, that's what attracted Butcher's audience. Some people will try his other series, but only a small number.

This is why author brand is important. If you like my military science fiction, then you're going to like my space fantasy. They use the same tone, and bear many similarities. If I take away the space setting though? Those readers will go find another science fiction author to read. Because they want space.

Knowing this, I can grow the audience I'm attracting, or I can grow multiple, separate audiences. Which sounds more profitable to you?

I have a post-apocalyptic author brand, a non-fiction author brand, and a science fiction author brand. In hindsight, I should have focused on either the science fiction or the non-fiction. The more I dilute my efforts, the less powerful each individual brand.

If I was going to branch out like I did, then I should have used a pen name for either the fiction or the non-fiction (much like Joanna Penn). Now that I've built the brand I have, however, I make sure to reinforce it as intelligently as possible.

Every time I release a book, or relaunch an old one, I ask if it builds my author brand. If it doesn't, I'll give it a makeover and maybe an omnibus, but that's it. The books will never receive a full relaunch, unless my author brand changes.

Exercise #3- What's your author brand? What genre do you want to be known for? Pick one, and start building around it. Use that brand on your website, social media, and in the front / back matter of your books.

Bonus: Define ways for your author brand to be present on all your books. Is your author name always the same font, size, and location? Do your titles all use the same colors, or font? What can you do to telegraph to your readers that all your books belong to you?

5

INITIAL ACTION PLAN

We now know whether or not your book is already profitable, and exactly how many copies we need to sell to hit our goals. We have some ideas of what we'll need to fix or replace. We're pretty sure that this relaunch fits our author brand. Still, what we're staring at is largely a pile of notes.

How do we go from that to a successful relaunch? Incrementally. It begins with your Initial Action Plan (IAP), which is basically just saying "I'm going to do these things, in this order." This is a list you'll refine over time, and it isn't something that stops after you run a promotion, or finish this relaunch.

Your backlist is long term. You'll likely relaunch the same book several times over your career, and the IAP is the foundation of that cycle. You may relaunch the same book or series again in a year, or in three. With the IAP, we're just conducting a single experiment, based on the needs of our specific book.

So, uh, what actions should we be taking exactly? How does one relaunch?

Types of Relaunches

Holy crap did it take us a long time to get to actual relaunches. We're finally there. Assuming your relaunch is on brand, you know what your book's problems are, and you know if it's profitable, you're ready to create your first experiment.

To do that, I've broken launches down into several categories. These are meant to be broad, and in some cases overlap. They're merely a guideline to provide a framework for you to structure different relaunches based on the needs of that individual book.

There's a sliding scale of effort involved in a relaunch. At one end you have a simple makeover, which will not cost much in the way of time, or money. On the other you have the Six-Million-

Dollar Book, where you get new covers, and give the book a thorough rewrite.

Below you'll find a brief description of each relaunch type. In the next few chapters we'll go over each in detail.

The Makeover
Time: Minimal
Cost: Minimal

This is the minimum viable relaunch, and is often the best choice if you have a large backlist. Every other relaunch starts with a Makeover, so the steps in this relaunch are always used.

Our goal with a Makeover is to overhaul marketing copy, categories, and keywords, and both the front and back matter of your book. We're after the low-hanging fruit, the stuff that can be quickly and easily swapped out or improved.

Once the Makeover is complete, we'll do a simple promotion, then put the book on autopilot using low-level advertising. If you have a large backlist, giving the whole thing a Makeover can have a powerful effect on revenue.

The Facelift
Time: Moderate
Money: Moderate

The Facelift builds on the Makeover, but also replaces the cover, and possibly the title. It may involve tightening the first section of the book, rewriting the sample portion until it ruthlessly hooks readers.

This takes time if you're rewriting, and money to replace a cover(s). It can work extremely well for authors with a rapid production schedule. If you don't have time to go back and rewrite a whole book, you can add a highly targeted cover, rewrite the first few chapters, tweak the blurb, and call it a day.

The Bundle
Time: Minimal
Cost: Minimal - Light

The Bundle works especially well for older series whose popularity has waned. You need to get new eyes on your book, and the easiest way to do that is by getting a book on the hot new releases list. An omnibus, collection, or box set does exactly that.

Beyond the few hours it takes to create the product page and the book itself, the author has to do almost nothing. Bundles rock, and can be used in conjunction with many other relaunches.

Costs are a little higher if you choose to have an original cover for your bundle. That may or may not make sense, depending on your needs.

The Six-Million-Dollar Book
Time: High
Cost: Moderate

Back in the mythical predawn of time, also known as the 70s, the most awesome TV show of all time aired: The Six Million Dollar Man. From that show arose the phrase "We have the technology. We can rebuild him." Steve Austin was rebuilt from the ground up, getting a new cybernetic body.

This relaunch does the same thing for your book, rebuilding it from the ground up. It includes a full edit, and possibly a full rewrite. It replaces the covers, and may even change the pen name / title of the book(s).

Your goal here is to take a book that missed the mark and turn it into a bullseye. Like the Bundle, you'll often end up with a new ASIN and another turn on the hot new releases list. You'll get this, because the Six-Million relaunch means unpublishing your existing book, then republishing as a new one.

The Big Splash
Time: Moderate
Cost: High

The Big Splash augments any other launch. Through liberal ad spending, and through cross-promotion with the other authors in your genre, your goal is to boost the relaunch into the stratosphere.

The Big Splash is generally reserved for authors who have money to burn, and who are fairly certain their relaunch has massive potential. It's big risk, big reward, and not a gamble most authors should take.

Exercise #4- This one will shock you. Consider all relaunch options. Which one(s) sound like they might work? Rank them in order of usefulness and efficiency. What sounds like the best use of your time and money? Can you get away with a Makeover, or do you need the full Six-Million?

Bonus: Consider what you'd need to change about this book to make it worthy of a Big Splash. Does the book you are currently writing have those same qualities? Why or why not?

6

THE MAKEOVER

Time: Minimal
Cost: Minimal

The Makeover is exactly what it sounds like. We're going to overhaul your book, to make sure every part is optimized. By the time we're done, this book will be a productive member of your backlist, efficiently earning a trickle of sales every day.

The process begins with the notes you took back in Chapter 1, but if you haven't done that exercise, use the *Deathless* case study from Chapter 2. I'll show you what I did, and explain why I did it.

Your goal is to examine the principles behind the changes, and then replicate those changes with your own book. Let's start by going back to the assessment steps. We're going to go through each, and make the appropriate changes.

Cover and Title

Changing a title means also changing the cover, and changing the cover is expensive. We're doing neither, because the goal of the Makeover is to increase revenue from this book without spending more money.

Blurb

Probably the most difficult part of the work we're doing for the Makeover is the blurb. We need to make that sales copy sing, to ensure that every word counts. Teaching proper copywriting is beyond the scope of this book, so I'm not going to try.

Instead, I've included an article I recently wrote. This article is designed to show you how to be economical with both prose and marketing copy. It teaches you to evoke questions, because questions are what keep people reading.

I know this is a little off topic, but the principles are useful. Here it is:

Every Words Counts

Hooking readers is both art and science. To capture their attention, distill your message to its essence. You have one sentence to evoke curiosity, and you do it by provoking questions.

1. *In eight seconds I will be dead.*
2. *When I die, my race dies with me.*
3. *That perfect, effortless smile would be the end of me.*

Why will the narrator be dead in eight seconds? Why will this person's race die with them? Why will a smile be the end of the narrator? We don't know, but we desperately want to. Lay your sentences like bricks, each building on the last.

1. *In eight seconds I will be dead. I pull the ripcord.*
2. *When I die, my race dies with me. I am the last.*

   3. *That perfect, effortless smile would be the end*
       of me. I bet it had been the end of every
       woman Brett had ever given it to.

Now we have a little context, but it only begs more questions. Why does this person have a parachute? Are they falling from a plane? Why is this person the last of their race? Who is Brett, and why does he have such an effect on the point-of-view character?

The third sentence is another brick. Lay it with care. Answer a question. Raise three more. Then lay another brick. Answer two questions. Ask three more.

   1. *In eight seconds I will be dead. I pull the*
       ripcord. Nothing happens.
   2. *When I die, my race dies with me. I am the*
       last. Fitting, as I was the first.
   3. *That perfect, effortless smile would be the end*
       of me. I bet it had been the end of every
       woman Brett had ever given it to. Of course,
       it wasn't the smile I was interested in.

Pull the reader forward, always craving more understanding. Then at the story's end, with the same care you placed the first brick, place the last. Answer the big question.

Subtly whisper three more.

Back to Branding

While the blurb might be the hardest part of the makeover, the branding section is the largest amount of work. We're going to be dotting a lot of I's and crossing a lot of T's. The goal is optimization—to make this book as effective as possible not just at selling, but at guiding people to your backlist.

We'll discuss the power of a backlist in Chapter 11, but in this section you'll begin to see how each book fits in with the others, forming an interconnected whole that guides your readers from book to book.

Keywords / Categories

Amazon allows us to use seven keywords for each book, and those keywords can either be search phrases, or specific keywords to get your book into additional categories. Which you choose depends entirely on your genre.

For *No Such Thing As Werewolves* I have three keywords that add categories, and four phrases people commonly search for.

For *Destroyer* all seven keywords are used to get into categories, because those categories provide a lot of exposure to overlapping audiences.

KDP support is often willing to add even more categories above and beyond what you can do with keywords. Ask politely, and you may be surprised. Just be certain you're only placing the book in the right categories. Quality trumps quantity, so only add more if they fit the audience you are trying to cultivate.

Front and Back Matter

This is where some of the magic begins to happen, and is the part I find the most fun. As you'll see in the case study, I really got creative with what I could add to the front and back matter of my books to drive readers to my other books.

At a bare minimum, you want to list your entire relevant backlist (all the other books in the same genre as this one). You also want to include a link to your mailing list, both in the front and back matter of the book.

A sample format might look like this:

Front Matter
Table of Contents
Other Books By You
Mailing List CTA (call to action)

Back Matter
Mailing List CTA
Note to the Reader
Excerpt of Next Book

Exposure

This is the part I screwed up most frequently, especially in the beginning. I knew I could run a Kindle Countdown Deal once every 90 days, so I did, even if I wasn't ready. Promotions should be used strategically, not on a timer. Your goal is to capitalize on the exposure promotions can generate, not to get exposure just for exposure's sake.

Retailers like Amazon reward success with more exposure. If your views to sales conversion is high, Amazon will reward you by showing your book to more people. That's why the preceding steps are so important. Your Makeover should ensure that as many people as possible click that buy button when they see your newly launched book.

So How Do You Promote Your Book?

Tactics differ from genre to genre, but there are commonalities across all of them. The cardinal rule of successful promotion? Go where your audience lives. Find where they congregate, and then find ways to get your book in front of them.

When I was first promoting *No Such Thing As Werewolves* I tracked down the biggest werewolf sites in the world. I approached each about advertising with them, and most were willing to create a banner ad. One of the biggest ran it for an entire month, and only asked me for $20. Sales poured in from that site.

Things have gotten more competitive since then,

and these days most successful authors have at least a small advertising budget. Right now I've allocated my daily spend between Amazon and Facebook ads, but in a year that could be BookBub and AdWords. Which platforms work changes very quickly, and I recommend focusing more on principles then on any particular platform. That platform that's working for you today? Tomorrow it's going to suck.

This is partly why I run so many experiments. I tried Twitter ads, YouTube ads, AdWords, and a host of other platforms. Most are ineffective, unless you invest large quantities of time and effort. I do it anyway, because when I finally find the effective platform, the money rolls in.

The trick with advertising is not to spend too much money, and to utilize it only after you have a book that you've optimized. Advertising a pre-Makeover book often means flushing your money down the toilet, because your conversion rate is so low.

If you make that book sing, though, then all of a sudden those ads become profitable. It takes fewer clicks to get a sale, and when you pay by click that's the holy grail.

A Note About Getting a BookBub

The 800-pound gorilla of the book advertising world is BookBub. This has been true for years, and is only more true with each passing month. BookBub understands how to use data to sell books, and this data-driven approach means they will almost certainly dominate the landscape for the foreseeable future.

The problem, as authors familiar with BookBub already know, is that it's nearly impossible to get a book selected. You submit, they decline. Over and over. It's discouraging, I know. But there are some things you can do to increase your chances, and these come straight from the people on the ground at BookBub.

I was fortunate enough to have a few drinks with two women from BookBub at the 2017 Smarter Artist Summit. Their advice made complete sense, and changed the way I approached submissions.

BookBub understands that the cover is the single most important selling point, followed by the title. Both are ruthlessly scrutinized, and BookBub chooses what they know will sell.

The example they used with me was Daniel Arenson's *Dragon War* Trilogy. Daniel's covers have dragons on them, and BookBub's fantasy readers LOVE dragons. Almost every time he submits those books, he gets accepted.

Contrast that to Daniel's *Earthrise* series, a series that has outsold every book I've ever written put together. BookBub won't touch it with a ten-foot pole, no matter how well it sells. Their data says their readers won't like it.

So how can we use this? Subscribe to BookBub for your genres, and look at the books that show up. Do this every day. Over time, you'll begin to notice patterns in the covers. You'll see what BookBub prefers.

The next time you do a Facelift, you'll be prepared to give it a cover BookBub will love.

Case Study: *Eradication*

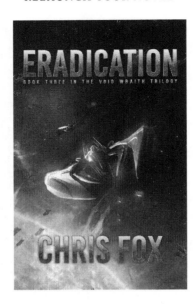

Eradication is one of my top selling books of all time, but the old girl is feeling her age. She's not selling like she used to, especially after her term in Amazon's Prime Reading program ended.

There's very little I need to do to clean her up for relaunch, and I loved being able to take a minimalist approach. I only needed to do three things:

1. Reformat the book
2. Add new front / back matter
3. Launch a Kindle Countdown Deal

The process began with reformatting, something I have neglected for entirely too long. Until recently, I'd always used Scrivener to export books. That resulted in clunky, ugly interiors. I've had weird problems where certain Kindle readers see incorrect fonts (usually terrible ones, like Courier).

Finally, I said "enough is enough" and invested in Vellum. Vellum is a software program that only runs for Mac, but there are equivalent ones for PC. The program allows you to quickly and effortlessly create a beautiful ebook. I used Vellum to make a version of *Eradication* I'm proud of...in ten minutes.

The resulting book looks amazing, and it's the same formatting I'm using for my books going forward. I want a uniform experience, so when readers pick up one of my books they know it.

I also took the time to adjust the front and back matter of the book, and this is where I got a little creative. I kept the usual front matter, but at the end of the book I included four chapters of *Behind The Lines*, the first book in my *Ganog Wars* trilogy.

Behind The Lines is basically a sequel to *Eradication*, but because they're separate trilogies there's no way for readers of *Eradication* to know that. At the time *Eradication* was written I hadn't even conceived of *Ganog Wars*, so of course there's no mention.

Now not only is there a mention, but fans can read a sample of the next book. This has resulted in dramatically increased sell-through, which is what we're all after.

Exercise #5- Give your book a Makeover. Take the blurb to author communities, and workshop it. Take a good long look at your front and back matter. What else can you add? Have you listed your other work? Can you give fans an excerpt of your next project so they know it exists?

Is your book in the right categories? Could you add more? Have you properly formatted it? Fix it. All of it.

Bonus: Schedule a Kindle Countdown Deal. Find three other authors in your genre who have a similar audience, and see if they'd be willing to announce the sale. In return, do the same for one of their books.

Research book sites in your genre. Vampires have ilovevampirenovels.com. What does your genre have? Find it, and advertise your KCD with that site.

7

THE FACELIFT

Time: Light-Moderate
Money: Moderate

The Facelift is the more intense version of The Makeover. You're doing all the same things, but you're also going to a deeper level. You'll almost always be replacing the cover, and you may need to change the title to fit the correct audience.

Time permitting, you may re-edit the first act of your book. You're finding and removing typos, and where possible you're improving the prose. It isn't a full rewrite, just a layer of polish.

Nor is that rewrite a definite must. You may find that what your book will most benefit from is new covers / titles, but that the writing itself is very strong. Go back to the notes you took from your assessment, then make your decision.

Replacing the Cover

Replacing covers is an expensive—and often terrifying—adventure. You really have no idea what the artist will produce, and I'm sure most of you know what it's like waiting an eternity to see if the artist can do your world justice.

Sometimes, those artists fail. It's heartbreaking. If this happens to you, I highly recommend not settling. Put the failed art away, and find another artist. This can be very, very expensive. I realize that. But I simply cannot overstate the importance of series branding.

Look at the cover of this book. If you've read any of my other books you knew immediately that I'd written this. That's the dream. You want recognition when your fans see your covers. They have to *know* it's you.

Before you replace the cover, you need to make sure the new one does this. When you look at the case study at the end of the chapter, note Rick's logic. He had good covers. He replaced them because the branding wasn't strong enough.

Now it is, and Rick makes the kind of living most of us can only dream about.

Finding a Cover Artist and Designer

Our notes say that our cover sucks, and we are now ready to replace it. But how do we do that, exactly? Where do we find someone who can create just what we need?

Assuming you've done the research in your genre, you now know which covers are doing well. Find one you especially like. Go to deviantart.com (or a similar site), and search for terms describing the image you like. If you write science fiction, search for starships. If you write Jane Austen Fan Fiction, search for Jane Austen.

You'll see an endless pile of images, most of them not at all what you're looking for. Somewhere in that mess, though, is exactly the gem that will bring your book to life. I spend several hours browsing like this, trying a variety of search terms I think are relevant. Eventually, I find what I'm looking for.

Most artists will say whether or not they take

commissions, and you're looking for the ones who do. They love getting emails from authors offering them work. I mean, wouldn't you? You prepare a brief of what you're looking for, give them some sample art and / or a mockup, and bam...you've got an original piece of artwork tailored to your novel.

What about the typography? Should you ask the artist to do that as well? Not unless you've seen other covers from the artist with amazing typography. I generally have an artist make the cover art, then turn that over to a designer. That designer chooses what part of the artwork to use, and what style of typography to use.

The end result is breathtaking covers that sell truckloads of books.

Replacing Titles

Changing titles doesn't always make sense, as you'll see in the case study. Sometimes, though, we have a situation like I do with *Deathless*. New titles are going to make a huge difference, because the existing titles are hindered by the tropes they use.

The beauty of operating in today's publishing landscape is that you can change your title at any time. If doing so proves to be a problem for any reason, you can always revert to the original title. You lose nothing in doing so.

However, it's important to consider the impact changing a title can have on an existing fan base. If you have a book that barely sold there's little risk, but if you sold a boatload of copies, then republish under a new title, people who read the original book are going to cry foul.

I always make sure to include a tag in the bottom of the description saying "this was originally published as X", and I would repeat that inside the front matter of the book.

Case Study: Rick Gualtieri

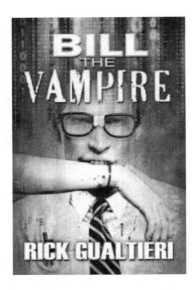

Original Cover

New Cover

Rick successfully relaunched the *Bill The Vampire* series, a eight-book comedic horror series with an ever-growing following. Rick's series was doing okay when he first started, but only after he gave it a Facelift did it begin to take off.

Rick didn't change the covers until after he'd launched book six of an eight-book series. Up until that point he had covers from four different artists; while they were nice, there was zero branding cohesion. Fans weren't immediately clear on which book was which, or if they were even in the same series.

So how much did it cost to replace six covers? A whopping $3,000. Rick did it anyway, because he knew the ebook market was changing. Gone were the days of publishing whatever you could produce in Photoshop. He needed tight branding, the kind that really draws the eye. Investing in his business made sense to him, and it paid off.

His new covers are amazing. If you look at the series page on Amazon, you'll notice that the covers are iconic, even as thumbnails. There is never any doubt in my mind that I'm seeing a *Tome of Bill* book when I look at one of the covers.

Rick says the change didn't have a dramatic

impact on sales at first. He didn't lose hope though. Rick kept experimenting. A few months later the new branding cohesion finally began to show results, and sales ticked up across all books.

Later, as a separate relaunch, Rick added a round of editing to clean up the books. Up until that point, the books had done well. In the four years leading up the relaunch Rick earned nearly a hundred and fifty thousand dollars from the series, a success by any measure. In the two years since the relaunch, the book has earned another **three hundred and fifty thousand dollars**, breaking the half million dollar mark.

Exercise #6- You guessed it. If you selected The Facelift, you're going to apply this to your relaunch. Go to Deviant Art and track down a new cover artist. Reach out to that artist with an email, or on Deviant Art.

Bonus: Find three artists. Get a sketch from each, and go with the artist who best captures your world.

8

THE BUNDLE

Time: Minimal
Cost: Minimal-Light

The Bundle is my absolute favorite relaunch, and I've used it twice already. I plan to use it again in a few more months. The concept is simple. Bundle the first few books in a series, and set them at an attractive price.

Buyers love getting a deal. They absolutely love it. Most buyers like to binge-read series, the same way you binge-watch Netflix. This is especially true if you reduce the price on the box set as part of a promotion. If you list a whole trilogy for 99 cents, as you can see in the case study, the results can be spectacular.

The best part? A bundle takes almost no time or money to create. All you need to do is create a new Scrivener file (or whatever format you use), and build the book from its component volumes. That generally takes me less than an hour, especially if I'm using the first book as a template.

After that, all you need is a cover. There are a ton of great templates out there, most completely free to use. You can either spend an hour tinkering in Photoshop, or hire someone to do it for you. Either way, your cover should be inexpensive to create. Even if you're getting original artwork, it only brings up the cost to moderate.

My first box set is the *Deathless Omnibus*. It's earned a little over $15,000, which includes the ebook and audiobook. I didn't bother creating a paperback, since it would have been massive.

My *Void Wraith* box set came out much more recently, and has earned about $6,500 in three months. In both cases, this is on top of all the money generated from each individual launch.

I've earned over $20k from two box sets, neither of which cost me more than $50 to put together. Bundles. Are. Awesome.

Use With Caution

I would offer a caveat, in case you're overeager like I was when I released *Deathless*. *Vampires Don't Sparkle*, the third book, came out in October. Sales were strong, but declined rapidly. By early December they had flatlined.

Desperate, I immediately created a bundle, and launched it the first week of January. The box set soared, but cannibalized sales of the third book. Very few people bought it, and instead sales shifted to the box set. This repeated with the *Void Wraith* books when I released the box set.

The Bundle may significantly impact sales on your existing books, so with *Void Wraith* I waited a full six months before releasing it. For my next series, I may increase that to nine months, or even a year.

Try to think long term when scheduling bundles, but don't be afraid to use them to plug gaps in your publishing schedule. My February and March would have been terrible if not for the *Void Wraith* boxed set.

Case Study: *Universe In Flames*

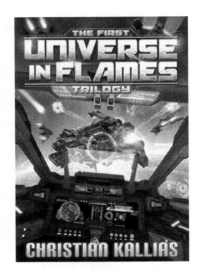

Christian released his box set the same week I released book one of the *Ganog Wars*. They're in the same genre. They have a similar feel. Our audiences are identical.

Guess which one fans purchased in droves? Christian's. Why? A thousand pages of fiction for a dollar? How can we say no? *Universe In Flames* sailed up the charts, hanging out in the #300 range for the first week, then sliding to #600 for the rest of the month.

Christian celebrated $400-500 days, every day,

the entire time. The tail is still carrying his books along, and hundreds of people are reading books 4-7 in the series. Christian's bundle took a series that was doing okay and made it into a powerhouse, generating five figures.

I took quite a few notes during Christian's launch, because it had never occurred to me to launch an omnibus with the same fanfare as a regular book. Now, I will make sure to always do that. Bundles can breathe incredible life into your backlist, and have almost zero investment.

Use them, and use them liberally.

Audio Box Sets

Once of the wonderful advantages of box sets is creating the audio. This can be expensive, but if you've already done it for the individual books it's as simple as using the existing tracks (as long as you have the rights, or the narrator agrees to the bundle). The *Deathless* box set has over 700 reviews on Audible. People buy it in droves, because it's 41 hours long.

As I've mentioned in previous books, Audible listeners are looking for the best value when they spend their credit(s). The longer your book, the more likely they are to buy. They're even faster than their ebook counterparts to snap up bundles.

I advertise my audiobooks separately from my ebooks, and do so quite profitably with the bundles.

Exercise #7- Has it been six months or more since you relaunched the first book in your series? If so, it's time for a bundle. Create one.

Bonus: Enjoy those sweet, sweet, bundle dollars.

9

THE SIX-MILLION-DOLLAR BOOK

Time: High

Cost: Moderate - High

The Six-Million-Dollar Launch, or Six-Million as I'll call it going forward, is the mother of all launches. You rebuild your series from the ground up, rewriting the terrible parts, and rebranding the entire thing to fit your new author brand.

Why would you go through all this trouble and effort? What if it fails? Big risk, big reward. If you can successfully pull off a Six-Million, your series that launched with a whimper can earn you your first five-figure month.

Or, it could flop. That's the reason I chose not to

do a Six-Million on my *Deathless* series. It's too much time investment right now, and I'm not willing to stake that much on the possibility of relaunching it.

Fortunately, Bryan Cohen was. His case study is one of the most interesting in the book, because we get to see what happens when you roll the dice.

How Much Rebuilding Are We Talking About?

You might have to rewrite the first book in your series from scratch, or replace half of it. You might have to do the same for books two and three in the series. The Six-Million is going to take a huge amount of your writing time, and that's on top of spending the money from replacing the covers.

I realize I'm painting this as scary. That's intentional. I don't recommend doing a Six-Million unless you're in a position where the series flopping wouldn't really hurt you. If you can survive it not doing well, but think that it will, then it may be worth the risk.

Someday, I'll take that risk for *Deathless*. For now, I'm sticking to newer, easier projects. When the time comes, *Deathless will* get new covers, a rewrite, and some sexy new thriller titles.

Case Study: Bryan Cohen

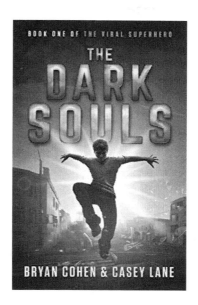

I've known Bryan for a long time, and I remember when he launched his *Ted Saves The World* Series. Bryan had just started The Sell More Books Show podcast, and garnered some early sales from his fan base.

That tail quickly fell off, and Bryan was disappointed with sales. He launched sequels, but the series never took off the way he wanted. Fast forward two years.

Bryan has become a much better writer, and has

mastered writing to market. He assessed his series, and came to the reluctant decision that it couldn't be saved with anything less than a full Six-Million. He needed to rebuild from scratch.

So Bryan rebuilt it. He re-wrote the first book literally from scratch, keeping only a few partial scenes. He added tighter pacing, a stronger plot, and better developed characters. Bryan made sure the first book hooked readers, as evidenced from the sell-through. The old book was 70k. The new book is 50k. Shorter, and much better.

Bryan shelled out about $2,500 for new covers, across five books. Those covers now look amazing. They're clearly branded, and the thumbnail conveys the scene well. He also used The Big Splash, dropping a full $4,000 on advertising. More on that step in the next chapter.

The blurb for the series was re-written, and the books he targeted were different. Bryan has truly found his niche, and the series is now earning more money than it ever has.

He also chose to completely redo the titles, and you can see why:

Old Titles

Ted Saves the World
Mind Over Easy
Portal Combat
The Light, The Dark, & The Ugly
Veil To The Chief

Silly, just like my Deathless series. New titles. More serious, better aimed at the average reader.

New Titles
The Dark Souls
The Telepath
The Candidate
Enemy Territory
The Devil Within

Bryan chose to release the first three books on the first day, then space out the last two for three weeks each to extend his stay on the hot new release list. This is a strategy I definitely agree with, and it also buys him time to write book six.

Bryan will have a seamless series of releases, each building on the momentum he's already achieved.

So how has his strategy panned out so far? *The Dark Souls* peaked at #451 in the store, and is hovering around #2,500 as of this writing. For contrast, *Ted Saves the World* peaked at about #2,500 and only if Bryan used massive promotion. Otherwise a high five-figure rank was normal.

I'd call that a massive success, especially since Bryan is charging $4.99 for all books in the series. Most people, myself included, have used a lower price of $2.99 on the first in series. Not Bryan. He's charging full price, and people are lining up to pay it.

This decision makes it easier to make a profit with advertising, and ensures that the readers he adds are trained to pay full price for his books. It's one I'm trending toward as well, as you saw in the previous case studies. If your work is good, people will generally pay a little more for it.

Experimenting with pricing can make you thousands of dollars a year. And, if you raise a price and sales drop, you can simply lower it again. Low risk, high reward.

Exercise #8- Before committing to a Six-Million, generate a timeline for the editing. How long is this going to take you? Add two more months, because you'll probably need it. Can you afford to invest that? If so, then flesh out your timeline.

When will you have the first book re-edited by? If there are other books, when will those be finished? Set some dates, and make the relaunch real.

Bonus: Brainstorm five new titles for your book that you think might better evoke the genre.

10

THE BIG SPLASH

Time: Moderate
Cost: High

I don't recommend the Big Splash for most authors, but I think it's something every author should at least be aware of. The Big Splash is very risky, and can cost you thousands of dollars if your market analysis is off.

The Big Splash is, quite simply, making the largest splash you possibly can. You want to get your book into the Amazon top #100? Or make a run for the USA Today list? This is how you do it. The Big Splash isn't complex, but it is more intricate than most launch strategies.

You will run a large daily spend of every type of ad you feel likely to sell even a few copies of your book. You'll beg, borrow, or steal mailing list swaps with other authors in your genre, especially big authors. You'll have a smart social media campaign, complete with boosted ads targeting your audience.

Pull every lever you can pull, so long as it has a chance to sell books to your target audience. This can get very expensive very quickly, but is often worth the effort.

If you launch your book high enough, and it sticks, you're looking at four figure days. The higher it sticks, the more profit you make. My most recent release, as you'll see below, stuck around #2,000 in the store. Not my best release ever, but it more than paid for the cost of advertising and production.

Every penny I make from now forward is pure profit, for it and the two sequels.

Case Study: *Ganog Wars*, Chris Fox

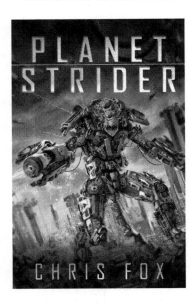

One of the crazier stunts I pulled on my YouTube channel involved writing three books in twelve weeks. I created *Ganog Wars*, the sequel to my *Void Wraith* trilogy.

I decided that for the release of the first book I'd use The Big Splash. Six other SF authors told their lists about the release, resulting in 200,000 sets of eyes landing on *Behind The Lines*.

I booked eReader News Today, Freebooksy, and a few other small sites. Then I turned on the ad spend. That ad spend started at $100 a day, ramping up to

$500 a day for the final three days. By the time the dust settled I'd spent:

$6,000 on covers and editing
$4,000 on advertising

A sweet $10k. Ouch. But you know what? I earned that money back by the end of the first thirty days, and that was before the audio was released. The book's rank peaked at #221 in the store, scoring the bestseller tag in every category.

The book was 99 cents for the first seven days, which dramatically cut down on the revenue I'd earned. That was painful, but I launched book two just 7 days after book one. That book was listed for $3.99, and sell-through was very high.

After the first week I raised the price, and the book fell to around #2,000. It's been falling ever since, and as of today, seven weeks from release, it's #7,023 in the store.

The final book in the trilogy releases just a few days after this writing, and I'll be running my first Kindle Countdown Deal for the full week. Hopefully, that will push the rank back up and expose another crop of SF fans to the now completed trilogy.

Even if it doesn't, my Big Splash worked. Perhaps not as well as I'd like, but it paid for itself and then some.

Again, I don't recommend The Big Splash for everyone. In fact, I recommend it to almost no one. But if you've reached a place where you want to hit the New York Times Best Seller list, or want to crack the Amazon Top 100, The Big Splash can get you there.

As of this writing, a mixture of BookBub, Facebook, and Amazon ads are a powerful cocktail for exposure.

Exercise #9- If you really want to go ahead with The Big Splash, begin making a list of every promo site you think would be worthwhile. Begin researching the authors in your genre, and use the list as keywords for Amazon, Facebook, and BookBub ads. What proportion you use those ads in is up to you, but your aim is to blast every network with your book.

It's vital that your ad spend be targeted, as discussed in *Six Figure Author*. Your whole goal is linking your book as tightly as possible to the top sellers in your genre.

Bonus: Reach out to the top three indie authors in your genre, and see if they'd be willing to do a mailing list swap with you.

11

THE POWER OF A BACKLIST

You're now familiar with the various types of relaunch. Hopefully, you've already got ideas on how you can apply one or more to your existing backlist. Before doing so, I want you to take a big step back and look at your backlist as a whole.

I want you to do this, even if you've only published one book. Picture yourself in five years, with thirty books. You've worked diligently on your backlist. Now it's time to manage it all.

Each book has two jobs. First, make sure that the reader buys it. That's most important, because if someone never reads the first book, they certainly aren't going to pick up the second. However, there's a second part that is more subtle, and nearly as important.

Every single book in your backlist must lead readers to your other books. This is the part where I fell down for so long, but now that I've made some changes I see the immediate benefit. My backlist went from a pile of books I hadn't looked at in a very long time, to a productive ecosystem working in harmony to earn me money.

I talk to many successful six-figure authors who focus more on new releases, just like I've been doing. We all lament our backlists, knowing that we should be doing something to drive sales to it. But we don't. We don't because we need to focus on new releases. It's a never-ending cycle—a cycle I've finally broken.

I've watched authors like Mark Cooper live for years off their backlist, only occasionally releasing a book. I finally understand how he's able to do that.

The Product Family Map

Managing a backlist is daunting, but it gets easier when you break it down into manageable chunks. The first step is creating your Product Family Map (PFM). On the surface, the PFM is a simple list of your books. But it's far more than that, as you'll see.

Your PFM is a kind of flow chart that shows which books lead readers to other books.

First, a bit about methodology. Using Yasiv.com I mapped out my entire backlist, seeing which books were connected to which. Next, I examined sales numbers during release months. Third, I checked Amazon's "Customers Went On To Buy" box located near the bottom of the sales page. Finally, I checked click-through rates on emails to different segments of fans. These data sources aren't statistically sound, but they're close enough to provide clues as to which fans will be interested in my other work.

Now, on the PFM itself. Let's use my backlist as an example. As you can see, I have two types of links. Strong, and weak. A weak connection indicates a trickle of sales, while strong has 50% or higher sell-through.

Void Wraith trilogy --> *Ganog Wars* (strong), *Project Solaris* (weak)
Ganog Wars --> *Void Wraith Trilogy* (strong)
Exiled --> *Void Wraith Trilogy* (strong)
Planetstrider --> *Ganog Wars* (strong)
Write Faster, Write Smarter --> *Void Wraith* trilogy, *Ganog Wars*, *Deathless*, *Project Solaris* (all weak)

Deathless --> Project Solaris (strong)
The First Ark --> Deathless (strong), *Project Solaris* (weak)
Project Solaris --> Deathless (weak)

People who find my *Void Wraith* trilogy are highly likely to buy *Ganog Wars*, and a few will buy *Project Solaris*. My *Ganog Wars* fans are highly likely to read *Void Wraith*, but unlikely to try any of my other fiction.

A trickle of fans from books like this one are apparently curious enough to try all my fiction. This is especially true of *Void Wraith* and *Ganog Wars*, which makes sense. I released videos showing the writing and editing of those books, and use both as examples in books.

Your goal when creating a PFM is to understand how fans flow through your backlist. Some series are cul-de-sacs. Some series are freeways, with exits at every other one of your other books. Once you understand which is which, you know where to focus your efforts.

Uh, Focus Which Efforts?

We only have so many dollars to advertise with, so we have to choose which books to allocate our precious budget to. The answer is always, always, always the books with the most strong links. You want to promote the books that will drive people to your entire backlist.

In my case, it works like this: I have about $25 a day in ads for *Destroyer*. People who read *Destroyer* buy *Void Wraith*, then *Eradication*. Most of them go on to buy *Behind The Lines*, then *Hold The Line*, and *Press The Line*.

A few of these people will also try *Project Solaris*, or *Deathless*. As I release new series, they'll check those out as well. The advertising dollars I spend on *Destroyer* are immensely profitable, because of the sell-through to other series.

Contrast that to *No Such Thing As Werewolves*. I have one $5 ad running each day, to ensure a trickle of sales. That's it. Until I overhaul the series, it simply isn't a good use of financial capital. People who read *Deathless* aren't interested in spaceships.

Multiple Points of Entry

My most popular series are the *Void Wraith* trilogy, and *Ganog Wars*. Both are trilogies, but they're basically a six-book series. I packaged them as trilogies for two reasons.

First, when I finish the third book, I can take a break to focus on other work.

Second, and more importantly, the first book in every trilogy is another entry point into my backlist. Many people found me through *Destroyer*, and were happy to buy *Behind the Lines*. Many more people bought *Behind the Lines*, then went back to read *Destroyer*.

I will be releasing two more trilogies in my *Void Wraith* universe, and when I'm done I'll effectively have a twelve-book series with four entry points. This gives readers a variety of ways to find me.

In a long series there's really only one way in, the first book. If the concept of the first book doesn't hook your reader, then they're probably not going to pick up the series. With trilogies, I have more chances to hook those readers. I can promote *Behind The Lines* in July, *Destroyer* in August, book one in the third trilogy the next month, and so on.

That's not to say I don't or won't write longer series. I think you should write the format that works best for you, as both can be very successful.

But it's important to understand the value of multiple points of entry.

Using Autoresponders With Your Backlist

Once you understand how fans flow through your work, you can begin crafting autoresponder sequences to capitalize on that. I know that people who sign up to the *Void Wraith* list should hear immediately about *Ganog Wars*. I also know that if I email them four weeks later telling them about *Hero Born*, a few of them will buy it.

I structure my autoresponders to gradually tell people about the books that I think they'll be interested in, and am very careful about who I tell what. I know that very few fans of *Ganog Wars* want to read *Deathless*, so when I mention it to them it's usually tied to another email, like an audiobook announcement. And I only do it once.

I never tell my non-fiction list about my fiction, unless a release is tied to something they care about. Both *Destroyer* and *Behind the Lines* were written on camera, showing how they went from concept to published. People who followed those challenges were invested in the books, and telling them about the releases made sense. But otherwise? Never.

Sending people emails about things they are not interested in weakens their relationship with you. Each time you do it, their trust is eroded. If that trust ever breaks entirely, they'll unsubscribe. Take care what you send.

Exercise #10- Yup, you guessed it. You're going to create a product family map. Jot down your entire catalogue of books. Now separate them by genre. Put an arrow next to each, and write in which books you think the first book will lead to (like so)

Book 1 --> Book 2 (weak), Book 3 (strong)

This is your model of how you think your backlist works. Some of it is probably right, and some wrong. Your job going forward is to constantly refine the model through research.

Bonus: Go to each of your book's Amazon product pages. Find the area where it says "Customers Went On To Buy." Use that information to strengthen your model for which books are leading to sales of the others.

12

PUTTING IT ALL TOGETHER

You've now learned the entire process for managing your backlist. Hopefully, you've picked a specific relaunch to use as your first experiment, and are already eagerly scrawling notes on how you're going to do that.

I'd say about 80% of you are. The other 20% are frustrated. I know this, because having now sold tens of thousands of these books to writers, I've learned that some people want more meat. They want a comprehensive, ironclad, always works system. Unfortunately, there is no such system.

The system that works is the one you yourself create. Books like this one can show you pieces that you integrate, but ultimately you need to craft a system that works for you. We all publish in our own way, and you should never accept what anyone says whole cloth. You should take what works, and discard the rest.

For that reason, I keep my books short. I don't sell worksheets or journals, because I want you to make your own journal. I want you to create your own spreadsheets. I want you to customize your system into the one that carries you to the loftiest heights of authordom.

But I also know how hard it is to find a starting point. So here's the recap of the steps that you're going to need to follow to manage your relaunch, stated one last time. This isn't the actual exercises; you can find those compiled at the end. This is just the broad steps.

1. Assess Your Book. Where did you screw up? Get yourself a pile of notes about the good, bad, and ugly parts of your book.
2. Pick a relaunch. Which experiment are you going to try?
3. Make whatever adjustments to your book(s) are required by the relaunch.
4. Relaunch the book as best you can.

You need to repeat 1-4 over and over and over. You want to relaunch your entire backlist continuously throughout your career. If you optimize your list, this will get easier and easier with time. It will also ensure that all your series continuously earn money...forever.

Every time you go through a relaunch, you're going to learn a ton. The first one, or first several, might bomb. Study each one carefully, and try to ascertain what you did wrong. Then do another relaunch with an eye for avoiding those same mistakes.

This industry is incredibly difficult. Competition grows daily. The only people who will make it long term are those who never stop growing and never stop learning. You need to experiment, and work diligently on your craft and your marketing.

The good news is that most people can't or won't do that. They won't continue to grow, and learn, and adapt. They'll quit. You aren't going to do that. You're going to keep after this, knowing that you're going to be publishing in a decade. In three decades.

Start building your systems today. You're going to need them.

The Inevitable Upsell

This year I gave a talk at the Smarter Artist Summit. Afterwards, many authors approached me to talk about the *Write Faster, Write Smarter* series. They had a variety of questions, and I did my best to answer them all. There simply wasn't time.

First one person, and then another, suggested that I start consulting. At first I was hesitant, but I received more requests, and by the time I flew home I had over a dozen. So I said *what the heck*. I had a one-hour Skype call with my very first clients, and they seemed pleased with the results.

I asked them to pay me what they thought my time was worth. They paid me a lot. Like way more than I ever thought I would get for an hour of my time. I started telling people that number, and much to my surprise many were willing to pay it.

I'm now consulting for about twenty people, and I'm happy to do it for you, too. If you're interested in having me take a look at your backlist, or help you with a launch, email me at chris@chrisfoxwrites.com. However, if you're considering it, first ask yourself this:

Are you really going to get that much out of a one-hour consultation? If you've read the books and done the exercises, then possibly. If you haven't? My books are $4. Read the books first and save yourself the money.

I've turned down more clients than I've accepted. If you're new at this, your money is best spent on editors that can help you improve your craft, and on covers.

If you're experienced and just looking to take it to the next level, give me a shout.

Additional Resources

Throughout the book you heard me repeatedly mention my YouTube channel. Not everyone is into video, but if you are I'd encourage you to check it out. I post a video every week, and have covered everything from how to outline your novel, to how to create an audiobook. For those reading the print version, you can find the videos at chrisfoxwrites.com.

There are also companion videos to this book, which you can find here. If you're reading the first version of this book those videos haven't gone live yet, so you aren't imagining the lack of a link. Check my YouTube channel and by the time you read this the videos will be live.

LETTER TO THE READER

This is, as usual, my favorite chapter to write. It's my open dialogue with you, something I've learned to treasure since putting out the first book in this series.

In Six Figure Author I used the stern tough-love tone, and I'm going to do that again here. I'll never stop being the wide-eyed dreamer who believes anyone can do this writing thing, but at the same time I'm not as naive as I once was.

I know that very few people will do the exercises in the next chapter. I know that most people who buy these books never even read them. I regularly get emails from people saying they just finished *Write to Market* or *5,000 Words Per Hour*; then they'll ask a question that I answered in the first chapter.

I'm not writing this chapter for those people. I'm writing it for you. I'm writing it for the person committed to making publishing work for them. My first year as a full-time author was one of the most stressful of my life. Yours probably will be too. If you've been full-time for a while, then you can tell us young'uns all about stress.

This business is hard. We have to constantly sell books, or we don't eat. The fact that you were a six-figure author yesterday doesn't mean you are today. We have to fight to keep what we've earned, and there are always setbacks along the way.

But here's the thing: It's all worth it. I wake up when I want to wake up. I go hiking, just because I need space to dream. I will never miss a family event again, because there's no one in the world who gets to tell me what to do for a paycheck.

My freedom is predicated upon selling books. Selling books is predicated on a large and efficient backlist. I work diligently every day to learn more about doing that. When I worked for a startup, 60-hour weeks were common. Now if I only work 70 hours it probably means I took a sick day.

The work never stops, and I often feel like I'm falling further behind. Thankfully, I have other successful authors to lift me up. I've made a lot of friends along the way, especially the crew over at the Author's Corner. We keep each other moving, and I think that kind of support system is necessary for creatives like us.

I don't know what stage of your author career you're at. I've met people who've been doing this for decades, and know more than a few that are about to push publish for the first time. What I do know is that you and I have a great deal in common. Getting this far, to the point where you worry more about publishing and less about "someday I want to finish a novel," that puts you in a breed apart.

We're professional storytellers, and I am proud to stand among you.

-Chris

EXERCISES

Exercise #1- This one won't surprise you. All the questions we asked earlier? Get out a sheet of paper, open a Word document, or get out your tablet. Answer all questions with as much detail as you can. Understand that some of the answers will require you to spend time researching. Or reading.

Try to spend at least a few minutes on each question, until you are satisfied you've answered it as completely as possible.

If this is something you don't yet feel comfortable doing, read the next chapter. My case study gives context on how you complete an assessment.

Bonus: Repeat this exercise for each of the books in a series you want to relaunch. Over time, we're going to relaunch them all. Understanding what you have to work with for your entire backlist will be very helpful as you read the rest of this book.

Exercise #2- Calculate ROI for the book / series you'd like to relaunch. How many copies do you need to sell to get this book into the black? If you're already in the black, how much do you need to make in order to consider this relaunch a success?

Bonus: Repeat this process for your entire backlist. Yeah, that can be a lot of work. It's totally worth it.

Exercise #3- What's your author brand? What genre do you want to be known for? Pick one, and start building around it. Use that brand on your website, social media, and in the front / back matter of your books.

Bonus: Define ways for your author brand to be

present on all your books. Is your author name always the same font, size, and location? Do your titles all use the same colors, or font? What can you do to telegraph to your readers that all your books belong to you?

Exercise #4- This one will shock you. Consider all relaunch options. Which one(s) sound like they might work? Rank them in order of usefulness and efficiency. What sounds like the best use of your time and money? Can you get away with a makeover, or do you need the full Six-million?

Bonus: Consider what you'd need to change about this book to make it worthy of a Big Splash. Does the book you are currently writing have those same qualities? Why or why not?

Exercise #5- Give your book a Makeover. Take the blurb to author communities, and workshop it. Take a good long look at your front and back matter.

What else can you add? Have you listed your other work? Can you give fans an excerpt of your next project so they know it exists?

Is your book in the right categories? Could you add more? Have you properly formatted it? Fix it. All of it.

Bonus: Schedule a Kindle Countdown Deal. Find three other authors in your genre who have a similar audience, and see if they'd be willing to announce the sale. In return, do the same for one of their books.

Research book sites in your genre. Vampires have <u>ilovevampirenovels.com</u>. What does your genre have? Find it, and advertise your KCD with that site.

Exercise #6- You guessed it. If you selected the Facelift, you're going to apply this to your relaunch. Go to Deviant Art and track down a new cover artist. Reach out to that artist with an email, or on Deviant Art.

Bonus: Find three artists. Get a sketch from each, and go with the artist who best captures your world.

Exercise #7- Has it been six months or more since you relaunched the first book in your series? If so, it's time for a bundle. Create one.

Bonus: Enjoy those sweet, sweet, bundle dollars.

Exercise #8- Before committing to a Six-Million generate a timeline for the editing. How long is this going to take you? Add two more months, because you'll probably need it. Can you afford to invest that? If so, then flesh out your timeline.

When will you have the first book re-edited by? If there are other books, when will those be finished? Set some dates, and make the relaunch real.

Bonus: Brainstorm five new titles for your book that you think might better evoke the genre.

Exercise #9- If you really want to go ahead with The Big Splash, begin making a list of every promo site you think would be worthwhile. Begin researching the authors in your genre, and use the list as keywords for Amazon, Facebook, and BookBub ads. What proportion you use those ads in is up to you, but your aim is to blast every network with your book.

It's vital that your ad spend be targeted, as discussed in Six Figure Author. Your whole goal is linking your book as tightly as possible to the top sellers in your genre.

Bonus: Reach out to the top three indie authors in your genre, and see if they'd be willing to do a mailing list swap with you.

Exercise #10- Yup, you guessed it. You're going to

create a product family map. Jot down your entire catalogue of books. Now separate them by genre. Put an arrow next to each, and write in which books you think the first book will lead to (like so)

Book 1 --> Book 2 (weak), Book 3 (strong)

This is your model of how you think your backlist works. Some of it is probably right, and some wrong. Your job going forward is to constantly refine the model.

Bonus: Go to each of your book's Amazon product pages. Find the area where it says "Customers Went On To Buy." Use that information to strengthen your model for which books are leading to sales of the others.

<<<<>>>>

71933780R00075

Made in the USA
San Bernardino, CA
20 March 2018